Single...

Now What?!

Josephine Tiberio

AuthorHouse™
1663 Liberty Drive
Bloomington, IN 47403
www.authorhouse.com
Phone: 1-800-839-8640

Published by AuthorHouse 05/08/2012

ISBN: 978-1-4772-0595-2 (sc)
ISBN: 978-1-4772-0594-5 (e)

Library of Congress Control Number: 2012908840

This book is printed on acid-free paper.

This book is dedicated to all my readers and to all the tears I've shed over the past years. May my readers find strength and renewal, and may my past tears be given a purpose!

Introduction

So you're currently single. It probably feels as though someone has suddenly ripped away a piece of you, and you're lonely. Your life has changed in a major way, and you're going to have a lot more free time on your hands. The time that used to be filled with that special someone now needs to be filled with something else. I have found that this is a major part of being able to not think of an ex constantly. You need to fill the time that was once spent with the ex with something that brings happiness to you. This will be different for everyone. What I find fun, you might never consider doing. This time is now about *you*! You are the only one who can take back control of your life and make yourself happy. Embrace being single. Life is all about choices, and we all make our own choices. Choose to be happy! You are the only one in control of how you feel; therefore, you must make a decision to be happy!

After a breakup, you may be feeling sad, which is fine immediately following the breakup, but now it's time to look forward. It's only normal to feel sadness after the loss of another person, but you must move past this. The world is full of wonderful opportunities! Tell yourself, "I deserve happiness." You need to get over the loss, so you can move on with your life. Moving on won't come fast and will take time, but soon you will not think of the ex as much.

It's only normal to go through the emotions of feeling sad, but you must realize that you need to break through the emotion to move on and be happy again. Happiness will come to you with time and some inner work on your part. You must focus on doing things that make you feel positive. This doesn't mean finding another partner to make you feel happy. It means finding happiness by just being you. You are a wonderful and beautiful being. Tell yourself this if you start to get in a negative mindset. Say to yourself, "I am wonderful. I am beautiful." Do this even if you don't feel that way. With time, it will work to positively shape how you feel about yourself.

I also suggest that you get rid of any remembrance of the relationship to save yourself some tears. This includes photos, jewelry, letters, phone numbers, etc. Find the ex's number and rid yourself of it. This will help you to not contact the person and drag out the breakup process. If you have it memorized or if your ex has a tendency to contact you, call your phone company and have the number blocked from your phone. You need to get a grip on your life and start the healing process. Ridding yourself of things that remind you of your ex will help you to move on. Such things could trigger a setback with the progress you are making. You need to surround yourself with positive things that trigger positive emotions. It's all about putting yourself in situations that trigger happy thoughts and feelings within you.

When you wake up in the morning, get ready for your day before your activities. Take a shower and get a fresh start to a new, beautiful day. Embrace the positive opportunities of a new day. Clean your face and wake yourself up. If you wear makeup, put your makeup on how you like it. It's all about doing what's going to trigger positive emotions within you. If you are dirty and stinky, you will feel dirty and stinky, which will trigger negative thoughts and feelings. So get yourself washed up and on a good track for having a positive day even if you don't feel like it. You have to fight for yourself, because no one else is going to be able to do this for you.

This book is an attempt to help you trigger positive feelings and thoughts within yourself. It is filled with activities to turn to when you need to come up with a way to fill time. You should not sit home and sulk. You need to get out and live your life! Life is too short to waste the days that you have. For some activities, you may want to take a friend with you, or you may just want to go by yourself. This is another thing to keep in mind as you go through this book. There is nothing wrong with going somewhere alone. It's actually a good way to do some self-reflection and become comfortable with just being yourself. With any of the activities listed, I do encourage you to travel responsibly.

Lastly, I have included affirmations to help motivate you. The affirmations can assist you with keeping positive thoughts flowing through your mind. You can refer to the book anytime you start to feel yourself having negative thoughts and/or feelings. Simply, choose an affirmation. Then repeat it within yourself or say it out loud. This type of self-talk promotes a healthy mind set. It is important to have positive thoughts within your mind, because they affect how you feel. An affirmation contained within this book is not directly related to the activity it may be paired with. The affirmations are written to be of use for any part of your day and with any activity. Choose whichever affirmations work for you. Try to remember at least one positive affirmation in your mind to refer to when you need a quick positive emotional boost!

** Live your life... and enjoy it! **

Today is a good day. *

Go to a Café

Cafés are a great place to sit and relax while enjoying a beverage and/or a tasty treat. Ask someone at the café if the business has a punch card or a saver's club, which can be a good way to save money. For example, some cafés offer punch cards that reward you with a free beverage after so many purchases. Being a part of a saver's card can offer you discounted pricing. While at the café, you can read, write, and/or go on the Internet if you have a computer with a wireless connection. You can also bring an iPod so you can listen to your own music. Some cafés may even have bands on certain nights, which can offer something different to go to. Another nice thing about a café is that you don't have to dress up, because it offers a relaxing atmosphere. You can just wear sweatpants and a sweatshirt if that makes you happy.

** I am awesome. **

Treat Yourself to Something Tasty

This may be a meal or some type of dessert that makes you happy. Eat the cake, cookies, or carbs that you want and feel good about it. I do encourage this activity in moderation.

** Today I am free to do whatever I want. **

Go on a Vacation

Go on an all-friends vacation or a singles vacation, but whatever you do, don't put yourself in a couple's situation. This will not help you to not think of your ex. You do not want to emotionally put yourself into a situation where it is you along with a bunch of people all coupled up. It will only put negative thoughts in your head about your own relationship situation. You need time with friends to laugh and have fun. If you don't have friends to go on a vacation with or would rather go somewhere by yourself, you could go on a singles vacation. You can sign up for a vacation with others who may be in a similar situation.

✻ I love myself. ✻

Have a Spa Day

Treat yourself to a day of relaxation. You could go on a spa vacation or simply make an appointment at a local spa. Most places offer various body massages, skin treatments, manicures, and pedicures.

* *I am strong.* *

Go Rock Climbing

Rock climbing can be a great way to release some energy. It can be fun and is a good source of exercise. It gets you out of the house and moving about . . . right up a mountain!

❋ The world has blessed me in many ways. ❋

Get a Manicure and/or a Pedicure

Just a simple manicure and/or pedicure can make you feel so much better. It feels good to have sexy hands and feet. When getting a manicure, you can upgrade it to a gel or shellac manicure. This form of manicure will last about two weeks as opposed to a few days.

** I enjoy and appreciate the free time that I have. **

Go Sledding, Skiing, or Snow Tubing

The winter months can tend to be depressing, because you are getting limited sunlight and spending more time indoors. If you enjoy the outdoors and/or want to try something new, then skiing, sledding, or snow tubing may be a great choice. Sledding and snow tubing are more cost-effective, because you just need to have a sled. Rental costs of ski equipment can be much more expensive. You can make a vacation or a day trip out of this fun activity.

** The world is a beautiful place full of opportunities. **

Go to the Beach

The beach can be fun and relaxing. There are so many fun things you can do on the beach. Some of them include tanning; participating in beach volleyball, surfing, or outdoor games; looking for seashells, snorkeling, swimming, etc.

** I love new activities. **

Go Fishing and/or Hunting

Even if you're not really an outdoor person, you can still find fun in this activity. You can go fishing and/or hunting with someone who is experienced. Some towns may require you to have a permit or license to fish and/or hunt. If you're the type of person who doesn't like the thought of harming another living thing, you could always use targets to shoot at. Hunting can involve guns, bow and arrows, harpoons, and more. You may need to receive lessons prior to beginning such an activity.

* *Life is wonderful, and*
I am a lucky person. *

Take a Cooking Class

Cooking classes can be a great way to start a new hobby. The classes also prepare you to have some cooking knowledge to impress a future partner. You can sign up for cooking classes by yourself or with friends.

** I deserve someone great, and
I will find him/her. **

Go on a Wine Tour

Wine tours are a fun way to spend a day. This activity typically involves more than one person. You can arrange a limo to pick up you and your friends to head to the wineries. There may also be breweries along your way!

✻ Things will get better. ✻

Have a Night Out with Friends

Have a night out with friends. A night out with friends can be fun as long as you do it responsibly and don't contact the ex via phone.

** I am fabulous. **

Sing Karaoke

Have a fun night out singing karaoke with friends. You can go somewhere that is having a karaoke night or have people over to sing karaoke. There are video games made especially for singing karaoke at home. It's an activity that you can do even if you can't sing well. In that case, you may feel more comfortable singing with a friend or a group of friends. The words are provided, so you have no need to worry about remembering the lyrics.

** I am a fighter, and I only depend on myself to make my dreams come true. **

Join a Gym

A gym can be a great place to release energy and stress. Exercise can help with managing stress, as well as making you feel healthier and better about yourself. Many gyms have a variety of classes to cater to most of the members' preferences.

** I am motivated. **

Join a Club

By joining a club, you can stay occupied with club activities. There is a club for every person. Joining a club allows you to share common interests with others. You may develop new friendships and learn new skills. Joining a club may require money if it is through an organization. You could also create your own club with friends for no cost.

** I am creative and have wonderful ideas. **

Get a Hobby

A hobby is a great thing to have. You could learn a new skill or continue one that you have always had. A hobby could be a sport, or maybe you are a collector. Some people prefer to write or make crafts. If your hobby is a craft, you could even think about turning to craft shows to make a profit from it. Craft shows can be a great way to meet new people as well.

** I don't care what others think of me.*
*I am awesome! **

Get a Tattoo or Piercing

If you choose to get a tattoo, I highly recommend getting something that makes you feel good about yourself. Get something that reminds you of yourself and your newfound strength. A tattoo should be used to symbolize courage, growth, and moving forward. A piercing can be a fun way to feel free and a little like a rebel. Tattoos are fun but permanent, so do not get anything that reminds you of your ex.

** Damn, I look good. **

Get a Makeover

Getting a makeover can just make you feel better. It can promote confidence and a sense of a new beginning. You can get a fresh start with a fresh, new you!

❊ I am making my dreams come true. ❊

Write

Writing is a great way to express yourself. You may wish to start a journal or maybe even write a book. Poetry can be a great way to use writing. Words to a new song can even be written and then placed with music. Use your experiences to make something magical.

** Everyone loves me, and I feel hot. **

Go Shopping

Shopping can be very therapeutic. It's nice to take time for yourself. There is something wonderful about looking at new designs and products that are on the market. Even if you don't buy everything you want, it's still a great way to treat yourself. You can go shopping and simply window shop for things you want in the future or buy something that you see that you like. Shopping can just be buying off of clearance or sales racks too. Shopping doesn't have to involve spending a ton of money.

** I have many positive things going for me. **

Go Bowling

You don't have to be a pro to go bowling. You can bowl by yourself or with friends. It can be a daytime or nighttime activity. Joining a bowling league is a great way to fill one night a week with a definite activity and an opportunity to meet new people.

* *Something new and great is coming.* *

Go for a Walk or Run

Walking or running can be a therapeutic activity while being healthy. Take an iPod with you if you prefer. Music can keep you motivated.

I love my life.

Go to a Theater

Take a night to get a ticket to the theater. You could see a play, ballet, opera, musical, etc.

I am moving forward.

Go to a Concert

Go online and see what local venues are bringing what types of concerts. Concerts can be an outdoor or indoor activity, so you can see them throughout the year. You may even consider traveling to see your favorite artist!

** I'm a winner. **

Go to a Sporting Event

Sporting events are held throughout the year. You can do something local or travel to see your favorite team. You can also participate in tailgating activities, which can be fun. Tailgating and then going to a game is a great way to occupy an entire day. To spice things up, you can wear something from the team you are cheering for.

** I control my own future. **

Go to a Psychic

A psychic can be a great way to seek clarity and hope about your life and future. Prior to going to one, you may want to get a reference if you know of someone who has had a good experience. Some people have mixed emotions about psychics, and if it isn't an activity for you, then it is fine to skip this activity. Only do activities that you feel comfortable doing.

** I have a beautiful life. **

Go to a Bookstore

Bookstores are a great place to do some self-reflection or to lose yourself in a book. If you choose to buy a book, select something that you enjoy. Try to get something that will make you happy and not sad. The self-help section can be helpful and allow you to do some self-reflection. Bookstores can also provide inspiration!

** I am going to have a good day. **

Go to a Gun Range

Going to a gun range may be a good release of energy. You will need to make sure that you have the proper training prior to shooting a gun. Call the gun range ahead of time, so you know what the procedures are prior to going. It may provide you with a drastically new experience to take your mind away from your ex. This activity can be a therapeutic way to release energy.

Warning: Only participate in this type of activity if you feel that you will not harm yourself or someone else. If you feel like you are going to harm yourself or someone else, you should immediately seek help from a doctor and/or therapist. I am not responsible for the actions of others.

I see every day as a gift, and I will appreciate today.

Paint

Painting can be very therapeutic. You can paint how you feel. You can take lessons or simply jump into it yourself. You could go to a local craft store and buy supplies. There are books on painting and lots of information online as well.

✻ I choose to be happy. ✻

Buy Fresh Flowers

Buy yourself flowers. You do not need another person to buy you flowers. Take back control of your life and do what makes you happy. If you like flowers, then buy yourself some! Go to the store and buy the flowers that you want. Get creative by mixing flowers together to custom make something magnificent for yourself. Fresh flowers can be a great addition to a room and bring cheer and life to your environment. Buy flowers that make you happy. If you like flowers being delivered, then go online and order some for yourself with a positive message attached to it. For example: You are beautiful; you are wonderful. Keep yourself smiling and never let anyone make you feel like you can't buy flowers for yourself.

** Every day is a blessing, and
I choose to enjoy today. **

Pray

Take time to pray. This may be through going to a religious gathering or simply asking for help. It's okay to ask for help. It may be a good time to get back to praying if you haven't done it in a while. If you already pray a lot, do not give up. It's important to remember that things could be worse. Do not hate God or the universe for anything that has happened to you. Focus on the good contained within any situation. You must have bad times in order to appreciate the good ones. No one gets through life without having a bad day or two.

** I am the only one who can make me happy. **

Meditate

Meditation can provide you with time to center yourself and regroup. You can do this with a group of people or by yourself. There are books on meditation, as well as audio technology that can help guide you through a meditation.

** I choose to laugh and smile. **

Gamble

Gambling can be a fun way to spend your time if you can control yourself with your money. This can be done at a casino or a bingo hall. You can make a casino trip with friends or go by yourself. Bingo is also a fun time, but you may need to contact local halls to see when game times are. You will want to arrive early to get a spot and make sure you don't miss any early bird games.

** I am in control of my own thoughts and feelings. **

Participate in a Religious Activity

Whether it's going to a church or a group ceremony, take some time for yourself to reflect and be thankful for your life. It's a good opportunity to stop thinking of yourself and think of others. Religious activities inspire you to be a better person starting from within yourself.

* *I love the way my place looks and feels.* *

Clean Your Home

Making your environment more organized and clean can help you feel better. It helps to promote better energies within your living space. It also can be seen as an opportunity for moving about and getting some exercise!

* *I can do anything I set my mind to.* *

Listen to Music

Listen to music that promotes positive feelings. Listen to music that talks about being a strong individual. Keep your music choices fun and happy. Dance and be carefree!

*** I enjoy my quiet time to myself. ***

Watch a Movie

You can watch a movie that you rent or go see one in the theater. Do not be ashamed to go to a movie on your own. If you want to go see a movie in a theater and it makes you happy, then no one has the right to tell you otherwise. It's no crime. Watch a movie that will generate happy feelings.

** I feel good about myself. **

Volunteer

Volunteering will most likely help you to feel better about being single while occupying your time. You will be given the opportunity to help someone, as well as the opportunity to appreciate your life. I recommend volunteering at a local hospital or nursing home. It's especially humbling if you get a chance to speak with someone with an illness who has a better attitude than yourself. Self-reflection and inner growth can take shape with this activity.

** I deserve someone who always makes me smile. **

Go to an Auction

Auctions can be a fun time if you're looking to buy something. There are a variety of types of auctions. They can sell anything—from cars to people! Auctions can be fundraisers for special causes as well.

** No one has the right to make me feel bad about myself, and I will not give anyone the power to do so. **

Go to a Museum or Gallery

A museum or gallery can be a great place to learn and even do some self-reflection. You may leave with a new perspective or understanding about life. This is an activity that you can do alone or with someone else, which is nice.

** It's all about me right now. **

Plant a Garden

Gardening can be a great activity. This doesn't have to be a flower garden. You could plant any type of garden you wish, such as a vegetable garden. It signifies helping something to grow, which is what you are doing with yourself. You have to get rid of the weeds to make room for the flowers to blossom. Gardens take work, but when they're complete, you'll have something beautiful to be proud of.

** I only need myself. **

Read a Book

Books are great, because there are many different kinds for all types of people. Books do not just have to consist of storybooks. They can be books to learn from, such as a hobby book or a self-help book. I suggest taking a stroll around a bookstore to see if anything catches your interest. You may be surprised what you stumble upon!

** Beauty is everywhere, and I choose to see it in all that I do. **

Go Horseback Riding

You don't have to own a horse to go horseback riding! Horseback riding can be a great activity to relax or to just have a fun experience. You can take lessons by yourself or in a group.

** I am so smart. **

Take a Class

A class can be a fantastic way to learn about something you have an interest in. This could be anything from an educational class at a school or even some type of Karate class. Classes are great, because they give you a planned activity to do each week. On days when you do not have your class, you can use time to study or practice. Such an activity will keep you busy so you don't have time to think about your ex!

** I choose to fight for myself. **

Lose Weight

Losing weight is something that can help build your confidence when you're getting back into the dating arena. It can also promote an I-can-and-will-do-better mentality. It can help refocus your thoughts to something productive. Losing weight can be a very difficult battle, but it's all about figuring out what works for you. There are programs that you can join if you need help, such as Weight Watchers. It may take several tries before you figure out what works for you.

** I am positive and attract positive things. **

Create a Visionary Board

A visionary board can help you to put your wants into perspective visually. The purpose of a visionary board is to positively focus on what you want to bring into your life. It's a board that consists of pictures or sayings that are positive. For example, if you want to find a partner who is happy, then you could put a picture on the board of a person that is happy. The board allows you to be creative and focus on positive changes. You can update and change your visionary board as your thoughts and life change.

** My life will come together **

Start a Scrapbook

Scrapbooking is a great activity that allows you to be creative while organizing photos (not of your ex—stay focused). This is an activity that you can do at your leisure whenever you have free time. It's a great way to fill up time. You can make a scrapbook for yourself or give a scrapbook as a gift. Craft stores allow you to get super creative with this activity. Some stores carry kits especially designed for scrapbooking, which can help if you don't feel you are creative.

** I make my own rules and am strong. **

Play Games

There is a lot of fun that can come from playing board games, electronic games, and/or card games. It is also a great way to get friends together. There are games that you can play by yourself, as well as ones that you can play with others from a remote location using the Internet. Games are great—they make you focus on what you are playing, because they require your attention to win!

** I will have positive thoughts today. **

Go to an Amusement Park

Amusement parks are jam-packed with excitement! You can go on rides and play games. On a hot day, you can go on water rides that provide an opportunity to cool off. There isn't any time for thinking about your ex when you're flying down a roller coaster!

** I am brilliant. **

Get a License or Certification

If you have wanted to get a licensure or certification of some type, now is a good time! You have extra time for studying and staying focused. You can use this as an opportunity to increase your pay or become a specialist in an area and teach a class or two! A wonderful hobby could turn into a great part-time employment opportunity!

** It's a wonderful thing. **

Decorate Your Living Space

Refresh your life with a living space that is new and fun! Focus your energy on making improvements to the world around you. Change your space in a way you have always imagined.

✻ I have a lot of love to give to the right person. ✻

Get a Pet

A pet can be a great companion as long as you're willing to take care of it. There are many types of pets that you can choose from (for example, a pet lizard or fish). If you are the type of person who doesn't have time to take care of a pet such as a dog, then you may want to get something that is more independent like a cat. You can take a walk through a pet store to decide what type of pet you would like to welcome into your home!

✼ I make my own life exciting. ✼

Go to a Rodeo

A rodeo can be full of excitement and may provide you with a new form of entertainment that you may not be used to. You can even add to the fun by getting festive. For example, put on some cowboy boots and a cowboy hat!

** I deserve happiness. **

Go Mudsliding

Gather up some friends on a rainy day and go sliding down a hill. It's messy, but it can be a blast of fun! Look online for examples of this!

* *I keep things hot and exciting.* *

Go Play on a Slip-and-Slide

Gather up some friends on a warm day and make your own slip-and-slide on a hillside. This can be a fun, wet, and wild time. Look online for how best you would like to create this with the resources you may already have.